PEOPLE POISONS

PLASTIC

BY

JOHN WOOD

Cavendish Square
New York

Published in 2023 by Cavendish Square Publishing, LLC
29 East 21st Street
New York, NY 10010

Edited by: William Anthony

Designed by: Danielle Rippengill

Cataloging-in-Publication Data

Names: Wood, John.
Title: Plastic / John Wood.
Description: New York : Cavendish Square, 2023. | Series: People poisons | Includes glossary and index.
Identifiers: ISBN 9781502663764 (pbk.) | ISBN 9781502663788 (library bound) | ISBN 9781502663771 (6 pack) | ISBN 9781502663795 (ebook)
Subjects: LCSH: Plastics--Juvenile literature. | Plastics--Environmental aspects--Juvenile literature.
Classification: LCC TP1125.W66 2023 | DDC 668.4--dc23

CPSIA compliance information: Batch #CSCSQ23: For further information contact Cavendish Square Publishing LLC, New York, New York, at 1-877-980-4450.

Printed in the United States of America

Image Credits

All images are courtesy of Shutterstock.com, unless otherwise specified. With thanks to Getty Images, Thinkstock Photo and iStockphoto. Cover: wow.subtropica, Rayyy, sokolovski, Milan M, Teerasak Ladnongkhun, Tinnakorn jorruang. Images used on every page – Rayyy, wow.subtropica. 4 – Khrystofor. 5 – LadyPhotos. 6 – MOHAMED ABDULRAHEEM. 7 – M.Somchai. 8 – Willyam Bradberry. 9 – Larina Marina. 10 – Again Peace. 11 – vwPix. 12 – Erlantz P.R. 13 – anyaivanova. 14 – Karel Bartik. 15 – Olha Rohulya, Rudmer Zwerver, Anan Kaewkhammul. 16 – Sundry Photography. 17 – Najmi Arif. 18 – Jao Cuyos. 19 – oneinchpunch. 20 – wavebreakmedia. 21 – Aleksandra Suzi. 22 – Huw Penson. 23 – Wutthichai Phosri.

CONTENTS

Words that look like <u>this</u> can be found in the glossary on page 24.

PLASTIC EVERYWHERE

This toy boat is made of plastic.

We use plastic to make lots of things, such as computers, phones, and bottles. Many toys are made out of plastic too.

Plastic is very useful. Sometimes it is made to be soft, like a plastic bag. It can also be hard, like plastic forks and spoons. But where does plastic go when we are done with it?

Plastic can be see-through, or it can be colorful like these plastic chairs.

The PROBLEM with PLASTIC

This landfill is full of plastic.

If plastic is not recycled properly, it can be very bad for the planet. Plastic doesn't completely break down and go away. This is a problem when it is dumped in landfills or in the ocean.

All of this plastic causes big problems for animals. They might get tangled in the plastic and become trapped, or accidentally eat it and die.

A monkey trapped in a plastic bag

POLLUTING the SEA

A lot of plastic ends up in the ocean. It can break into smaller and smaller pieces and become dangerous to all of the animals.

A turtle might eat a plastic bag because they think it is a jellyfish. This can choke them.

Plastic often washes up on beaches too.

If an animal gets trapped in plastic, it can make it harder to find food and **survive**. Pieces of plastic can also get stuck in the animal and hurt them.

WHAT IS MICROPLASTIC?

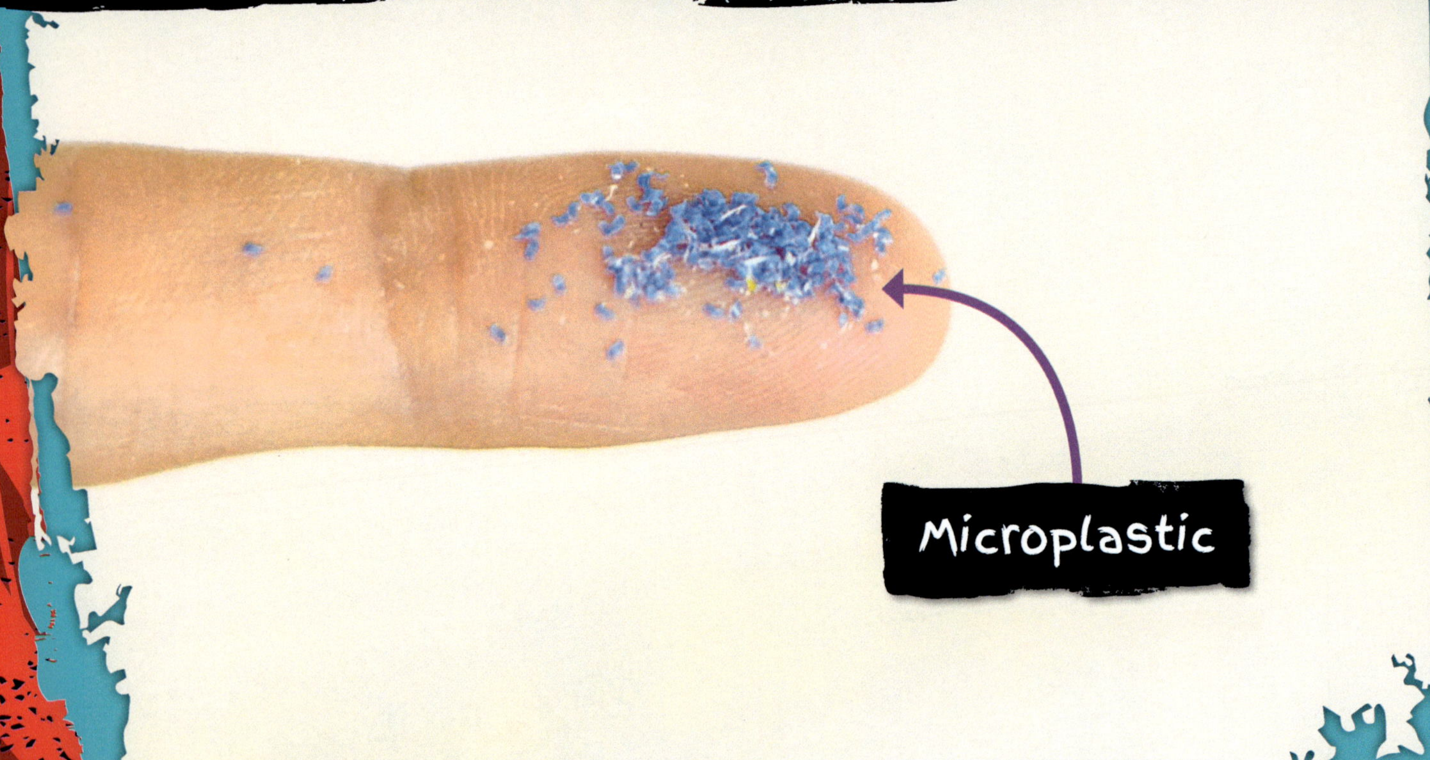

When plastic breaks down into very small pieces, it is called microplastic. Microplastic is very dangerous to animals and people.

Microbeads are another type of microplastic. Microbeads are added to things such as toothpaste or face washes. These small microbeads can get into the ocean and can be eaten by small animals.

Microplastic has been found everywhere in the world, from the highest mountain to the deepest point in the ocean. Not only is plastic dangerous for animals, but it could be dangerous to people too.

Every year, 8.8 million tons (8 million tonnes) of plastic are put into the ocean.

Plastic has been found in over 100 **species** in oceans, lakes, and rivers.

Microplastic is sometimes too small to see. It is in the water we drink, the air we breathe, and the food we eat. Plastic can leak **chemicals** into the ground, or into our food and water.

Plastic pollution is found throughout the food chain. But what is a food chain?

The FOOD CHAIN

Food chains show what animals eat. They often start with plants, which get energy from the sun. Herbivores are animals that eat the plants. Carnivores eat other animals.

Here is a simple food chain you might find in the woods.

Animals might eat plants and other animals with plastic inside them. This is how microplastics travel up the food chain. This can be bad for people because we are part of the food chain too.

An INVENTION to CLEAN the SEAS

An Ocean Cleanup project boat

The Ocean Cleanup project uses an **invention** that looks like a giant floating barrier. The barrier drifts along the waves, collecting plastic that will eventually be taken out of the ocean by boats.

So far, the Ocean Cleanup project is mainly trying to clean an area of the Pacific Ocean known as the Great Pacific Garbage Patch.

The Great Pacific Garbage Patch is an island of garbage that is three times the size of France.

This is called the Interceptor. It is cleaning up a river in Asia.

GETTING PLASTIC OUT of the OCEAN

Inventions such as the ones used by the Ocean Cleanup project are very good at collecting big pieces of plastic. However, small pieces of plastic are a lot harder to clean up.

These people are picking up plastic off the beach to recycle it instead.

It is important to act quickly to clean up our world. We need to use less plastic and make sure it is recycled or thrown away properly.

STOP PLASTIC POLLUTION!

You could also see if there are any eco-friendly projects at school that you can join in with.

Here are some things you can do to help stop plastic pollution and keep our planet clean and safe.

Make sure you recycle as much plastic as you can. Ask a grown-up if you are unsure whether something can be recycled or not.

You might have different bins for recycling at home.

Try not to use plastic at all! Ask your grown-ups to buy reusable bags instead of plastic bags. Can you get paper straws instead of plastic ones? Can you think of any other plastic that could be replaced?

These toothbrushes are made of bamboo.

If you are finished with something plastic, can you turn it into something else instead of throwing it away? A plastic bottle might make a good planter!

GLOSSARY

chemicals	things that are usually made by scientists
eco-friendly	something that doesn't damage or harm the natural world
energy	a type of power, such as light or heat, that can be used to do something
invention	a new machine or tool made by humans
landfills	places where waste is buried
pollution	harmful and poisonous things being added to an environment
recycled	used again to make something else
species	a group of very similar animals or plants that can create young together
survive	to continue to live

INDEX